250/

This book belongs to:

Spandanbyrch

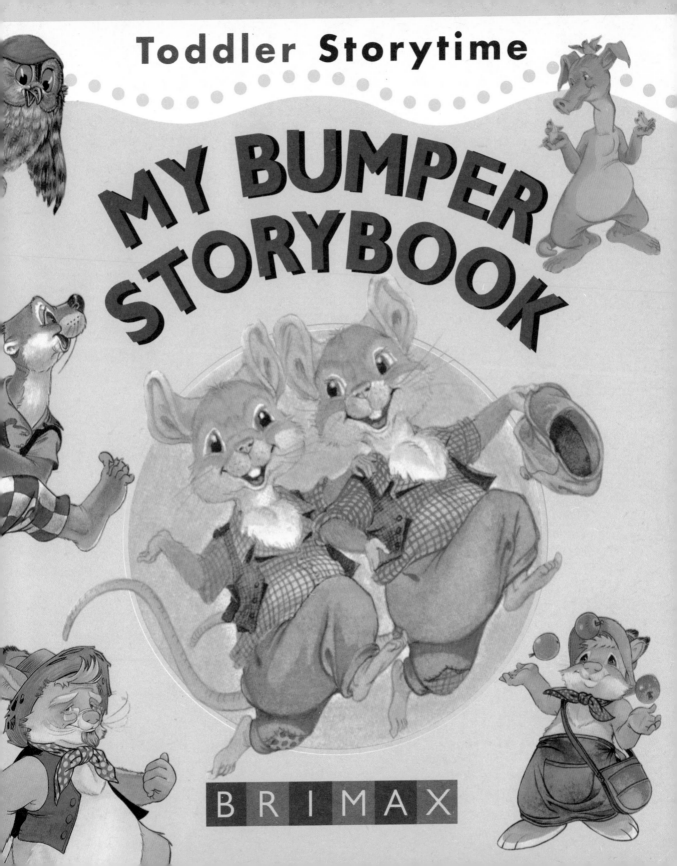

Toddler Storytime

MY BUMPER STORYBOOK

BRIMAX

First published in 2001 by Brimax
an imprint of Octopus Publishing Group Ltd
2-4 Heron Quays, London, E14 4JP
© Octopus Publishing Group Ltd
Printed in Spain

CONTENTS

SNOOZE AND SNORE

Snooze and Snore are twin mice who live
in Moss Hollow on Sunshine Hill.

They are very sweet but are little rascals
who cannot help getting into trouble.

Mrs Mouse is baking a cake in the kitchen. Snore dips a finger in the mix.

"Don't!" cries his mother. "Wait until I have finished. Then you can scrape the bowl."

Mrs Mouse puts the cake in the oven.
Then she lets the twins have the bowl.

Somehow they spread cake mix all over their noses and whiskers and the floor.

Mrs Mouse scrubs the floor and the twins' faces until they shine. Then she says,

"I need cherries for the cake. Can you
go to Mr Otter's store for me please."

The twins scurry down Sunshine Hill. Mr Rags, the scarecrow, waves as they pass.

Mrs Otter finds some cherries on the shelf. Snooze puts them in the basket.

It is hot walking back up the hill, and the twins sit down for a rest half way.

A hungry wasp flies into the basket. He wants to taste the cherries in the pot.

"Go away," says Snore. "Those are not for you." He waves his cap at the wasp.

The wasp takes no notice. Snore shakes
the basket and then swings it around.

Suddenly the basket, cherry pot, and wasp fly into the air and land on Mr Rags.

"Thanks! I need a new hat," says Mr Rags,
beaming as the cross wasp buzzes away.

"Where is my basket?" Mrs Mouse asks. Snooze and Snore explain as they sit down to eat delicious iced cake.

"What a story!" laughs Mrs Mouse. "Well, I shall just have to ask for my basket back and give Mr Rags my old bonnet."

Hop the Frog

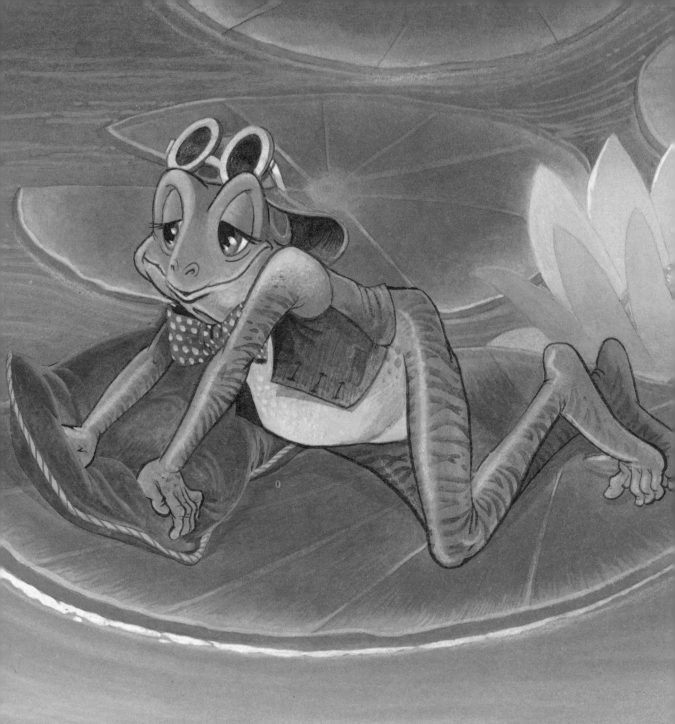

Hop the Frog has sleepy eyes, a wide grin and long legs that he likes to stretch out.

He lives in the pond below Sunshine Hill
and he enjoys snoozing on the lily pads.

But today every time he goes to sleep,
someone seems to wake him up.

First the little ducklings rush past making ripples and waves that shake the lily pad.

Then Tom Toad dives into the pond, and big drops of water splash all over Hop.

"Oh dear!" says Hop. "I must find a quiet place to snooze. This pond is too busy."

Hop hops out of the pond and hangs
a cobweb hammock in the reeds.

Soon he is dozing happily as the
hammock swings gently in the breeze.

The otter family arrive at the little pebble beach by the pond for a picnic.

"Catch!" says Mrs Otter, throwing an orange to Ollie. Ollie misses.

Wham! The orange flies straight into the
reeds and lands on Hop's tummy.

"Ouch!" yells Hop, tumbling out of the hammock. "Am I to have no rest today?"

Hop hops up Sunshine Hill. He yawns and curls up in a sunny spot by a mossy bank.

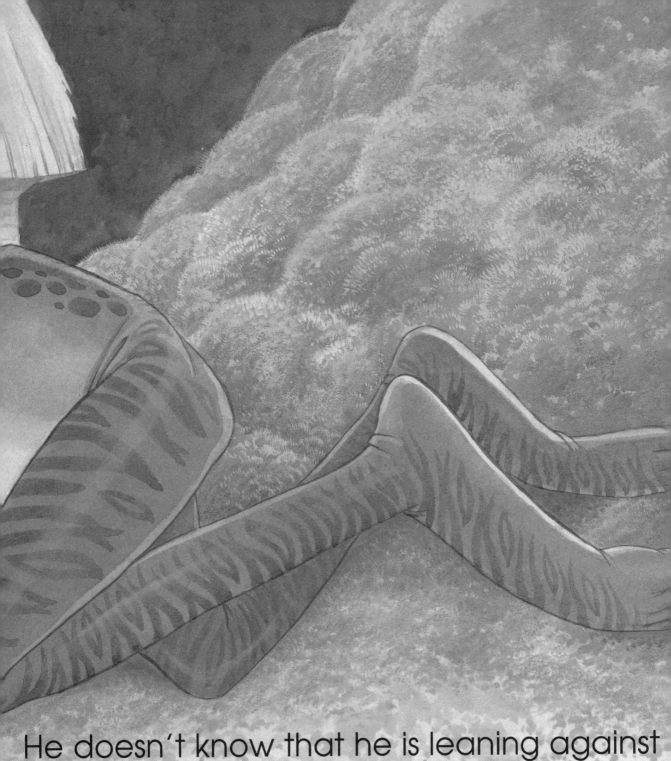

He doesn't know that he is leaning against a front door. This is where the mice live.

"What a lovely day for a walk!" says Mrs Mouse. She flings open the door.

Hop is sent flying. He rolls all the way down the hill and splashes into the pond.

"I think," says Hop, "I'll stay awake from now on. It might be safer." He plays all day with the ducklings and Tom Toad.

Then when the moon rises, Hop settles on his lily pad and sleeps so soundly that he does not even hear the owl hooting.

Ollie Otter

Ollie Otter has huge, shining eyes, cheeky whiskers and a big, wide grin.

He lives in the shop at the bottom of
Sunshine Hill and delivers baskets of food.

One day he goes down to the stream to take fresh bread and butter to Mrs Duck.

He finds his little toy boat in the basket
and decides to sail it in the stream.

Dibble, Dab and Dot the ducklings
waddle up to watch.

The boat sails along. It sails past the
reeds, under a bridge and into the lake.

"What a fine boat you have there, Ollie,"
say the frogs as the boat sails past them.

"Wait for us! Wait for us!" quack the ducklings, paddling hard to catch up.

There is a sudden, sharp gust of wind. The
boat spins around in a circle and then...

with a whoosh, it sails to the far side of
the lake and disappears.

Ollie cannot cross the lake. He has lost his boat. He rides home feeling very sad.

Mr Otter is having a quiet afternoon fishing. He feels a tug on the fishing line.

"A-ha!" he says. "I have caught a nice,
fat fish for supper!" He pulls in the line.

And there dangling on the end is Ollie's little, wooden boat. Mr Otter laughs.

"What a funny fish! But I know someone who will want it far more than fish pie!"

Ollie is moping. "I'm not hungry," he says. "I want my boat back."

At that moment Mr Otter walks in the door. "Look what I have!" he says. In one hand he holds up a fine catch of fish.

In his other hand is Ollie's boat. All the
otters cheer - and then settle down
happily to a delicious feast of fish.

Dibble, Dab and Dot

A lovely, splashy stream winds through the meadow at the bottom of Sunshine Hill.

This is where Dibble, Dab and Dot the ducklings come out to play each day.

Dibble is bossy. He quacks the loudest and always tells his sisters what to do.

Today he says, "Mr Rags needs a new hat. Shall we make one for him?"

"How?" say Dab and Dot. Dibble thinks hard. "I have an idea," he quacks.

He leads his sisters out of the stream and over to Mr Otter's store.

They buy some bright paper and string
and sticky tape.

The ducklings waddle back to the bank
and settle down to make the hat.

It is difficult. The tape sticks to their beaks
and the string wraps around their feet.

Then it rains. The paper gets wet and
tears. "This is hopeless," cry Dab and Dot.

"I have an idea," says Dibble. "Let's visit
Mrs Mouse. She will help us."

The mouse family are keeping dry inside
Moss Hollow.

"Come in out of the rain," says Mrs Mouse. "What can I do for you?"

Dibble says, "We want to make Mr Rags a new hat, but I think we need your help."

"I was going to give Mr Rags my old hat,
but making one will be much more fun."

Mrs Mouse helps the ducklings and her twins cut out some shapes from felt.

She sits at her sewing machine and makes a smart, new hat. Then they all stick the shapes on and put a feather on the top.

The rain stops. They take the hat to Mr Rags. He smiles and says, "It is just what I wanted. Thank you."

LITTLE DRAGON

Little Dragon in the Wood

One day, the animals in the
wood see someone
strange.
"Who is coming?" say the
birds.
"Who is coming?" say the
rabbits.
"It is a Little Dragon!" say
the bees.
The animals are frightened.
They all hide.

Little Dragon is hot.
He sits down on a log.
The animals can all
see Little Dragon -
but he cannot see them.
They are hiding.

What will Little Dragon do? He shuts his eyes. He opens his mouth. Little Dragon begins to sing. The animals do not like Little Dragon's song. They want him to stop singing.

The animals come out from their hiding places.
"Stop!" say the birds.
"Stop!" say the rabbits.
"Stop!" say the bees.
Little Dragon stops singing.

"Where have you come from?" asks Little Dragon.
"We live here," say the birds.
"I didn't see you," says Little Dragon.
"We were hiding," say the bees.

"Can I sing a song for you?"
asks Little Dragon.
"No! No! Please don't sing!"
say all the animals.
Little Dragon looks sad.
"Nobody will let me sing,"
he says.
Little Dragon begins to cry.
The animals have never
seen a dragon cry before.

"Are you a real dragon?"
ask the animals.
Little Dragon shows them
that he is. He puffs smoke
and breathes fire. The
animals are frightened.
They run away.
"Come back," calls Little
Dragon. "I will not hurt you.
I just want to sing."

"We will help you," say the birds. "Listen to us."
Little Dragon listens to the birds. Then he opens his mouth and tries to sing like the birds. But he can't! He puffs smoke and breathes fire.

"Stop!" say the birds.
"Stop!" say the bees.
"Stop!" say the rabbits.

Little Dragon is sad.
He walks away.
"Come back," say the
rabbits.
"We will help you," say the
bees.
"How?" ask the birds.
"We can hum," say the
bees. "Humming is like
singing."
The bees begin to hum.

"Can I do that?" asks Little
Dragon.
"You can if you try," say the
bees.
Little Dragon tries to hum.
He can do it! He can hum
just like the bees!
"Hum hum hum," hums
Little Dragon.
Nobody tells him to stop.

Little Dragon is humming a song. The bees are humming too. The birds are singing. All the animals join in. The rabbits tap their feet. The flowers nod their heads. Everyone is happy.

Dragon and the Rabbits

One day the baby rabbits come to see Little Dragon. "We want to learn to hum," they say.
Little Dragon shakes his head.
"You must go home to your mother," he says. "She will worry if she cannot find you."
The baby rabbits hop away into the wood.

Little Dragon is humming
again. The bees are
humming too. Along comes
Mother Rabbit.
"Where are my babies?"
asks Mother Rabbit.
"I told them to go home
to you," says Little Dragon.

Mother Rabbit calls her babies. They do not come. Mother Rabbit begins to cry.

"I have lost my babies," she says.

"Do not cry," says Little Dragon.

"We will find your babies for you," say the bees.

Little Dragon and Mother Rabbit look for the baby rabbits. The bees help too. The baby rabbits have gone. Nobody can find them.

"They must be hiding," says Little Dragon.

Then Little Dragon stops.
He stands still.
"Listen!" he says. "I can
hear something."
"So can I," says Mother
Rabbit.
"So can we," say the bees.

Little Dragon peeps over
the bush. Mother Rabbit
and the bees look too. They
see the baby rabbits sitting
on the grass.
"What are they doing?" ask
the bees.
The baby rabbits are trying
to hum. They are trying very
hard. But they cannot do it.

"Hello!" says Little Dragon.
"What are you trying to do?"
The baby rabbits see Little Dragon. They hop away and hide.
"Come out of there," says Little Dragon.

The baby rabbits will not come out. They do not see Mother Rabbit.

"Come out of there at once!" says Mother Rabbit.

"Yes, Mother," say the baby rabbits.

"Come with me," says Mother Rabbit. "We're going home at once." The baby rabbits look very sad.

"What were they trying to do?" ask the bees.

"They were trying to hum, like us," says Little Dragon.

"We can show them how to hum," say the bees.
"Yes," says Little Dragon.
So they follow Mother Rabbit.
It takes a long time to show a rabbit how to hum. Little Dragon tries very hard. So do the bees. At last the baby rabbits can do it.

Little Dragon is humming.
The bees are humming.
The rabbits are humming.
"I didn't know rabbits could hum," says Owl.
"My babies are the only rabbits that can," says Mother Rabbit.

Dragon's Hiding Place

One day, Rabbit comes to
see Little Dragon.
"What is wrong?" asks Little
Dragon.
"There are men in the
wood," says Rabbit.
"What do they want?" ask
the bees.
"They want Little Dragon,"
says Rabbit.

Little Dragon is afraid.
"What can I do?" he says.
"You must hide," says
Rabbit.
It is too late. The men see
Little Dragon. They run after
him. Rabbit gets under their
feet. He trips them up. The
bees buzz around the men.
Little Dragon gets away.

Little Dragon looks for
a place to hide. He sees
a hole in a tree. He gets
into the hole.
"What are you doing?" asks
Badger.
"I am hiding," says Little
Dragon.
"I can see you," says
Badger.
"What can I do?" asks Little
Dragon.

"Men are coming. They want to put me in a cage," says Little Dragon.

"I will help you," says Badger.

He rolls logs in front of the hole. Nobody can see it now. Nobody can see Little Dragon either. Badger goes home.

The men come. They have
a net. They have sticks.
"Where is that dragon?"
say the men. Little Dragon
keeps still. The men do not
see him. They go away.

It is safe. Little Dragon can come out. But where is he hiding? Nobody knows. The animals look for Little Dragon. Nobody can find him.

Little Dragon is still inside the tree. He knows it is safe to come out. He cannot get out. He cannot move the logs.

"I will shout," says Little Dragon. "The animals will hear me."

Little Dragon opens his mouth. But he knows he must not shout. He is a dragon. Dragons spit fire when they shout. Fire will burn the tree.

"I know what to do," says Little Dragon.

Little Dragon begins to hum. He hums as loud as he can.

"Hum hum HUM HUM!" Little Dragon's friends hear the humming.

"Only Little Dragon can hum like that," say the bees. "He must be inside the tree."

The animals try to move the logs, but they are too heavy. Badger comes along.

"There is nobody in that tree," says Badger.

"Yes there is," says Rabbit.

"Little Dragon is in the tree. We can hear him humming."

"Little Dragon is our friend," say the bees. "It is safe for him to come out now."
"Then I will help you," says Badger.
He helps to roll the logs away from the tree. Little Dragon comes out of the tree.
"I'm glad to see you all," says Little Dragon.
"We are glad to see you too," say his friends.

Little Dragon and Sleepy Owl

Little Dragon has many friends in the wood. Owl is one of them. Owl is awake all night and sleeps during the day. Little Dragon waves to Owl as he flies home.

But Owl is not happy. All the animals want to talk to him during the day. Owl is very tired. He cannot work day and night. He must get some sleep. Owl goes to see Little Dragon.

"Will you stand under my tree?" says Owl. "Then no one will come to talk to me. I must get some sleep."

"I will help you sleep," says Little Dragon.

So Owl goes back to his tree and Little Dragon stands under it.

A mouse comes to see Owl.
Little Dragon growls. The
mouse runs away.
A squirrel comes to see
Owl. Little Dragon growls.
The squirrel runs away.
Little Dragon growls when
anyone comes near the
tree.

"Are you asleep, Owl?" asks Little Dragon.

"No," says Owl.

"Why not?" asks Little Dragon.

"Your growls keep me awake," says Owl.

"I'm sorry," says Little Dragon. "What can I do?"

The bees know what to do.
They know a sleeping song.
"Hum hum hum," hum the
bees. "Close your eyes. Go
to sleep."
"Hum hum hum." Little
Dragon hums too. "Close
your eyes. Go to sleep.
Hum hum hum."

Owl's eyes are shut. Owl is asleep.
"Do not stop humming," say the birds. "Owl will wake up if you do."
Little Dragon keeps on humming. So do the bees.

The animals listen to the song. They get sleepy. The birds listen to the song. They get sleepy. Soon they are all asleep.

The bees are awake. The bees are still humming. Little Dragon is still awake. He is still humming. The bees are getting sleepy. Little Dragon puts his paws over his ears.

The bees are asleep. Little Dragon is still wide awake. His paws are over his ears. Little Dragon cannot hear the sleeping song.

Owl wakes up.
"I cannot hear anyone,"
says Owl.
Little Dragon tells him they
are all asleep.
Owl laughs when he sees
everyone. He laughs so
much that everyone wakes
up. And then they all laugh
too.

GRANDPA AND ME

Pipkin Rabbit is staying with his Grandma
and Grandpa. They live in Long Grass Lane.

Grandpa is digging the potato patch.
Pipkin is helping.

Grandpa is hot. He takes off his hat.
"I can hold it for you, Grandpa," says Pipkin.

Pipkin puts the hat on. It is too big.
He can see his toes but that is all.

Now Pipkin tries to dig with Grandpa's shovel.
It is too heavy. He falls over.

Grandma and Grandpa have a surprise.
They give Pipkin two packages.

There is a hat inside one package.
There is a shovel inside the other package.

"Grandpa looks like a big Pipkin and Pipkin looks like a little Grandpa," laughs Grandma.

"Where shall I dig?" asks Pipkin.
"You can clear the weeds from Grandma's flower bed," says Grandpa.

Grandpa is busy. He does not watch what Pipkin is doing. Pipkin is busy too.

Weeds and flowers look the same to Pipkin.
He digs them all up.

"Oh dear!" says Grandpa, when he sees
what Pipkin has done.

"I was trying to help," sobs Pipkin.
"I know," says Grandpa, drying Pipkin's tears.

Grandpa sorts out the flowers and the weeds.
He puts the flowers back where they belong.

The flower bed is full of flowers again but it is full of footprints too.

"We must clear those footprints away," says Grandpa. Grandpa lets Pipkin do it.

All the footprints are gone. Pipkin sees
Grandma coming. He hides in the long grass.

Grandpa tells Grandma what has happened.
"Oh dear!" says Grandma. She calls Pipkin.

"I am sorry, Grandma," says Pipkin.
"Please let me keep my shovel."

"Of course you can," says Grandma.
Pipkin is happy now. He gives Grandma
a big kiss.

A Windy Day

It is a windy day. Grandma is washing sheets.
Pipkin is helping her.

"The wind will soon blow the sheets dry,"
says Grandma.

Grandma is waiting for the next peg.
"Can you go a little faster?" she asks.

Grandma is called away. There are still two
sheets left to hang up. Pipkin has an idea.

Pipkin asks Grandpa to help.
"This is not as easy as it looks," says Grandpa.

The wind is playing tricks. It is pulling at the pegs. The pegs are getting loose.

The wind blows very hard.
The pegs fly into the air like birds.

Pipkin can see what is going to happen.
"Look out, Grandpa!" he shouts. He is too late.

Before Grandpa can move, a flying sheet
wraps itself around him.
"Help!" shouts Grandpa.

The more Pipkin tries to untangle Grandpa,
the more tangled Grandpa gets.

Grandma screams. She thinks Pipkin
is fighting with a ghost.

"Don't be afraid," says Pipkin. "It's only
Grandpa."
"Get me out of here!" shouts Grandpa.

Grandma takes charge.
"Keep still," she says to Grandpa.
"Unwind that way," she says to Pipkin.

"Are you all right?" asks Pipkin.
"I think so," says Grandpa.
Grandma takes the sheet to wash it again.

"Look up there!" gasps Pipkin.
"What shall we do, Grandpa?"

Grandma will be cross if she sees the sheet
on the roof. They must do something quickly.

"Hurry up!" whispers Pipkin.
"I am hurrying!" whispers Grandpa.
Grandpa has hidden the sheet.

Grandpa makes sure the sheet will not blow away again. He pushes the pegs down very hard.

The wind cannot pull the pegs off.
Grandma cannot pull the pegs off either.
Pipkin goes to get Grandpa.

"How did your sweater get like that?"
asks Grandma. Grandpa and Pipkin know,
but they are not telling.

The Tunnel

Pipkin and Grandma are picking berries.
Grandma knows where the best berries grow.

It is very quiet. The only sound is the buzzing of the bees.

Suddenly there is another sound.
"I can hear someone crying," says Pipkin.

"Unhook me please," says Grandma.
"Look over there," says Pipkin.

"We have just come across the road," says Mother Rabbit. "And Bobby has got left behind."

Poor Bobby. He is too little and too
frightened to cross the road by himself.

Mother Rabbit cannot leave her babies by themselves. She does not know what to do.

"Leave this to me," says Grandma.
"Shout if you see anything coming, Pipkin."

Pipkin is glad Grandma and Bobby are safe.
Everyone else is pleased too.

Pipkin tells Grandpa how brave Grandma
was. Grandpa looks very thoughtful.

Pipkin and Grandpa are busy.
"That looks like a good idea," says Grandma.

"Can we start digging now?" says Pipkin.
"The sooner the better," says Grandpa.

Everyone stops to ask what Grandpa and
Pipkin are doing.
"Look at the plan," says Grandpa.

Everyone wants to help. Everyone goes home to get something to dig with.

The hole is getting deeper. It is changing into a tunnel. Where is it going?

The tunnel gets longer and darker. Grandpa
hangs up a lantern to give some light.

Digging is hard work. Everyone gets thirsty.
Grandma comes with drinks on a tray.

Finally the tunnel is finished.
"Hello Grandma!" shouts Pipkin.

Now everyone can go under the road
instead of over the road.

Now even the smallest rabbit is safe.

Apples for Sale

The apples on the apple tree are ripe.
It is time to pick them.

"I will hold the ladder steady," says Pipkin.

Grandpa is going to sell some apples.
First he must put up a stall.

Grandpa takes the apples out of the barrel.
Pipkin puts a shine on the apples.

"Grandma is calling me," says Grandpa.
"I will look after the stall," says Pipkin.

"Apples for sale!" shouts Pipkin.
He hopes someone comes along soon.

Everyone comes to buy apples.
Pipkin is very busy.

Grandpa is gone a long time.
Pipkin sells all the apples.

Little Tom has run a long way.
"Can I buy one of your apples?" he asks.

"Is there one left in the barrel?" asks Tom.
"I will look," says Pipkin.

Pipkin stands on his tiptoes. He can see an apple. He cannot quite reach it.

"I have it!" shouts Pipkin. And then
he falls head first into the barrel.

The barrel wobbles. It falls over.
It begins to roll. Pipkin is still inside it.

Grandpa hears Tom Rabbit shouting.
Grandpa comes running.
"What is wrong?" shouts Grandpa.

"Stop! Stop!" shouts Grandpa.
"Stop! Stop!" shouts Tom Rabbit.

"I would if I could!" shouts Pipkin from inside the barrel.

"Where am I going?" shouts Pipkin as he
flies into the air.

"Into the pond!" shouts Grandpa.
What a big splash Pipkin makes!

Pipkin is wet and very dizzy.
But what is he holding?

"This is the best apple I have ever tasted,"
says Tom.
"Well done Pipkin!" says Grandpa.